GARFIELD

Whatever!

D1392667

JIM DAVIS

ℛℛ
RAVETTE PUBLISHING

First published by Ravette Publishing 2010.

Printed in the UK by CPI Bookmarque, Croydon, CR0 4TD
for Ravette Publishing Limited,
PO Box 876
Horsham
West Sussex RH12 9GH

ISBN: 978-1-84161-330-7

WHAT'S WRONG WITH YOU?

MY BRAIN IS STUCK IN HICCUP

YOU ARE WEIRD

JPM DAVPS 7-26

JIM DAVIS 7-27

JIM DAVIS 7-30

CLICK

JTM DAVJS 8-6

JIM DAVIS 8-29

WELL, IT WASN'T EASY,
BUT I GOT BOTH SHOES
ON THE SAME FOOT!

IS IT ANY WONDER I
SLEEP 18 HOURS A DAY?

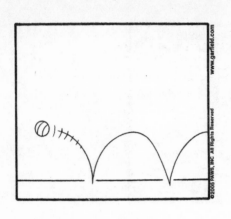

SLUP

HOW'S THE COFFEE?

IT GOT THE JOB DONE

JIM DAVIS 9-19

Distributed by Universal Press Syndicate

OTHER GARFIELD BOOKS AVAILABLE

Pocket Books	**Price**	**ISBN**
Am I Bothered?	£3.99	978-1-84161-286-7
Compute This!	£3.50	978-1-84161-194-5
Don't Ask!	£3.99	978-1-84161-247-8
Feed Me!	£3.99	978-1-84161-242-3
Get Serious	£3.99	978-1-84161-265-2
Gooooal!	£3.99	978-1-84161-329-1
Gotcha!	£3.50	978-1-84161-226-3
I Am What I Am!	£3.99	978-1-84161-243-0
I Don't Do Perky	£3.99	978-1-84161-195-2
Kowabunga	£3.99	978-1-84161-246-1
Numero Uno	£3.99	978-1-85304-297-3
S.W.A.L.K.	£3.50	978-1-84161-225-6
Talk to the Paw NEW	£3.99	978-1-84161-317-8
Time to Delegate	£3.99	978-1-84161-296-6
Wan2tlk?	£3.99	978-1-84161-264-5

Theme Books		
Creatures Great & Small	£3.99	978-1-85304-998-9
Entertains You	£4.50	978-1-84161-221-8
Pigging Out	£4.50	978-1-85304-893-7
Slam Dunk!	£4.50	978-1-84161-222-5
The Seasons	£3.99	978-1-85304-999-6

2-in-1 Theme Books		
All In Good Taste	£6.99	978-1-84161-209-6
Easy Does It	£6.99	978-1-84161-191-4
Lazy Daze	£6.99	978-1-84161-208-9
Licensed to Thrill	£6.99	978-1-84161-192-1
Out For The Couch	£6.99	978-1-84161-144-0
The Gruesome Twosome	£6.99	978-1-84161-143-3

Classics		
Volume One	£7.99	978-1-85304-970-5
Volume Two	£7.99	978-1-85304-971-2
Volume Three	£7.99	978-1-85304-996-5
Volume Four	£7.99	978-1-85304-997-2
Volume Five	£6.99	978-1-84161-022-1
Volume Six	£7.99	978-1-84161-023-8
Volume Seven	£5.99	978-1-84161-088-7
Volume Eight	£7.99	978-1-84161-089-4
Volume Nine	£6.99	978-1-84161-149-5
Volume Ten	£6.99	978-1-84161-150-1
Volume Eleven	£7.99	978-1-84161-175-4
Volume Twelve	£7.99	978-1-84161-176-1
Volume Thirteen	£6.99	978-1-84161-206-5
Volume Fourteen	£7.99	978-1-84161-207-2
Volume Fifteen	£5.99	978-1-84161-232-4
Volume Sixteen	£5.99	978-1-84161-233-1

Classics (cont'd ...)	Price	ISBN
Volume Seventeen	£7.99	978-1-84161-250-8
Volume Eighteen	£6.99	978-1-84161 251-5
Volume Nineteen	£6.99	978-1-84161-303-1
Volume Twenty	£6.99	978-1-84161 304-8

Gift Books	Price	ISBN
30 years - the fun's just begun	£9.99	978-1-84161-307-9
Don't Know, Don't Care	£4.99	978-1-84161-279-9
Get a Grip	£4.99	978-1-84161-282-9
I Don't Do Ordinary	£4.99	978-1-84161-281-2
Keep your Attitude, I have my own	£4.99	978-1-84161-278-2

Little Books	Price	ISBN
C-c-c-caffeine	£2.50	978-1-84161-183-9
Food 'n' Fitness	£2.50	978-1-84161-145-7
Laughs	£2.50	978-1-84161-146-4
Love 'n' Stuff	£2.50	978-1-84161-147-1
Surf 'n' Sun	£2.50	978-1-84161-186-0
The Office	£2.50	978-1-84161-184-6
Zzzzzz	£2.50	978-1-84161-185-3

Miscellaneous	Price	ISBN
Colour Collection Book 3 (new)	£11.99	978-1-84161-320-8
Colour Collection Book 2	£10.99	978-1-84161-306-2
Colour Collection Book 1	£10.99	978-1-84161-293-5
Treasury 7	£10.99	978-1-84161-248-5
Treasury 6	£10.99	978-1-84161-229-4
Treasury 5	£10.99	978-1-84161-198-3
Treasury 4	£10.99	978-1-84161-180-8
Treasury 3	£9.99	978-1-84161-142-6
How to Draw Garfield & Friends (May 2010)	£3.99	978-1-84161-384-5

All Garfield books are available at your local bookshop or from the publisher at the address below.

Just send your order with your payment and name and address details to:-

Ravette Publishing Ltd
PO Box 876
Horsham
West Sussex RH12 9GH
(tel: 01403 711443 ... email: ingrid@ravettepub.co.uk)

Prices and availability are subject to change without notice.

Please enclose a cheque or postal order made payable to **Ravette Publishing** to the value of the cover price of the book/s and allow the following for UK postage and packing:-

70p for the first book + 40p for each additional book
except Treasuries & Colour Collections... when please add £3.00 per book